CONTENTS

All words marked in **bold** can be found in the glossary

WHAT ARE THE SENSES?

When you wake up in the morning do you feel the warmth of your bed, switch off the alarm, look at the sunlight, listen to sounds in the house and sniff for breakfast?

All these actions involve your senses. People and animals have five senses: sight, hearing, smell, touch and taste. They use their senses to receive messages from the world around them. These messages give useful information such as whether there is danger at hand, if food is available or even if other people or animals are friendly.

People usually see certain groups of bright colours as attractive. Advertising agencies use bright colours to draw the eyes of possible customers to their products. In the natural world, bright colours may have developed for display purposes, or to serve a warning. Can you think of any types of brightly coloured plants or animals?

Which picture represents which sense? (Touch is shown by two pictures).

SECRET MESSENGERS

Your eyes, ears, tongue, nose, fingers and **skin** are at work all the time, picking up information from the world around you. Even as you sleep, they send sense signals to your **brain**.

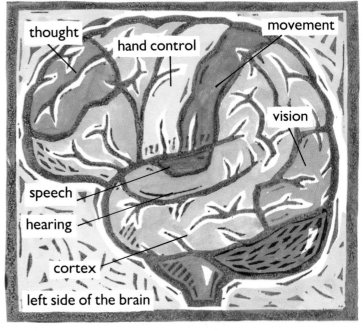

thought

hand control

movement

vision

speech

hearing

cortex

left side of the brain

▲ The brain's wrinkly outer layer is called the cortex. Messages from your tongue, eyes, ears, nose and skin pass along **nerves** to special areas of the cortex, each concerned with a particular sense.

Look at the strawberries on this page. A message travels from your eyes to your brain. The brain then sends signals to the rest of your body and your mouth starts to water and you feel hungry.

Your brain will grow until you are about 20 years old. The nerve **cells** will then begin to die and will not be replaced. Even so, plenty of cells will be left.

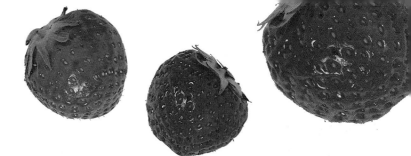

▲ Puppies cannot see when they are born. They use their strong sense of smell to help them nuzzle their way to their mother's milk.

▶ Take care before touching hot things. Nerve endings in your skin at once send alarm messages to drop things that could harm you. Signals from the left side of your body travel to the right side of your brain, and vice versa. The left side of the brain is bigger in most people: they are **right-handed.** The right side is larger if you are left-handed.

SIGHT

Only a small part of your eye can be seen from outside your body. The eyeball is actually the size of a ping-pong ball, set back into the skull. Every few seconds, your eyelids blink, covering your eyes with salty fluid. This helps to keep the eyeball moist and removes any dirt and dust which may get in. Your eyebrows stop **sweat** from your forehead running into your eyes.

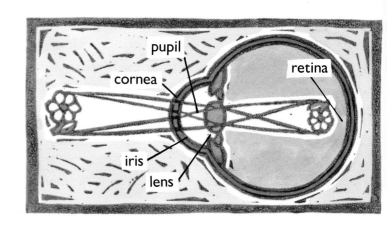

▲ Light reflected from an object enters the eye through the **pupil**. A **lens** focuses the image upside-down on to light-sensitive cells on the **retina**. The brain turns the image right side up.

▲ Your two eyes see things from slightly different angles. The brain joins the two images to make a '3-D' picture to judge depth and distance.

A chameleon can swivel its eyes round in their sockets, or even turn one eye forwards and the other one backwards. The chameleon can see in two different directions at the same time, which helps it watch out for danger.

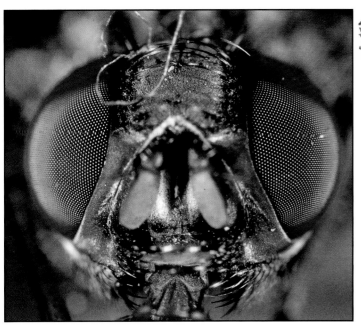

Hawks have very keen vision so that they can spot prey moving on the ground far below.

◀ A single fly's eye is a compound of thousands of tiny eyes, each of which takes in a separate view of an image. The fly's brain produces a mosaic from all the different images.

▲ Draw pictures in red and green. Make some cardboard spectacles with one red lens and one green lens from coloured acetate. Look at your pictures with one eye closed, then the other.

◀ Put a variety of objects on a tray. Ask a friend to look at the objects for two full minutes, then cover the tray with a cloth. How many things can your friend still remember? Now you try. Which of you can remember more of what you saw?

DARK AND BRIGHT

The coloured **iris** controls light entering the eye by changing the size of the pupil, the hole at the front. In dim light, the pupil gets larger to let more light in. In bright light, the pupil gets smaller.

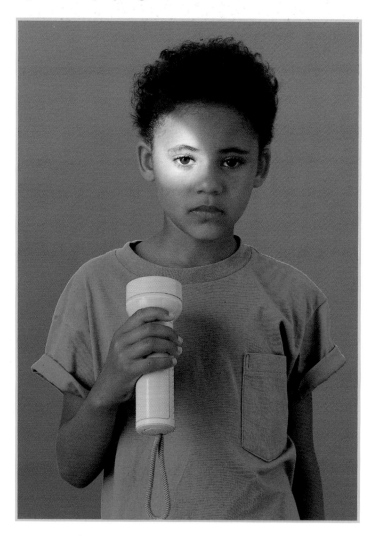

▲ Giraffes have good eyesight to watch for danger on the flat plains as they nibble leaves at the tops of trees.

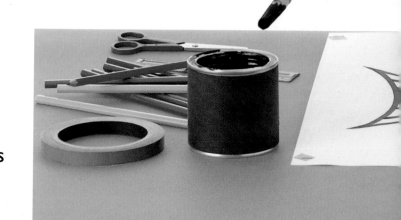

▲ Turn off the light and draw the curtains in a room. Point a torch so that a little light falls near the face of a friend. Look at one of your friend's eyes. How big is the pupil? Shine the torch nearer to the eye. What happens? Look at the other eye. The torch is not pointed at this eye and its pupil is still enlarged.

10

▶ In sunlight, a cat's pupils are narrow slits. At night, a reflective layer at the back of the eye sends back light to the sensitive cells so that extra light signals reach the brain. Cats can see much better in the dark than people can.

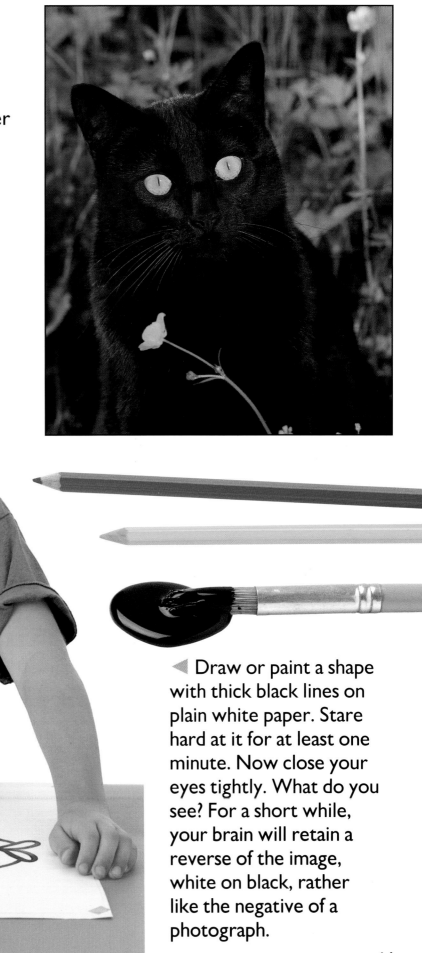

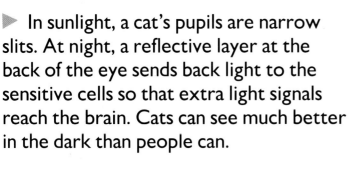

◀ Draw or paint a shape with thick black lines on plain white paper. Stare hard at it for at least one minute. Now close your eyes tightly. What do you see? For a short while, your brain will retain a reverse of the image, white on black, rather like the negative of a photograph.

SMELL

Your nose is very sensitive. It can detect many thousands of different smells. You also use it to take in air for your **lungs** to breathe in and out.

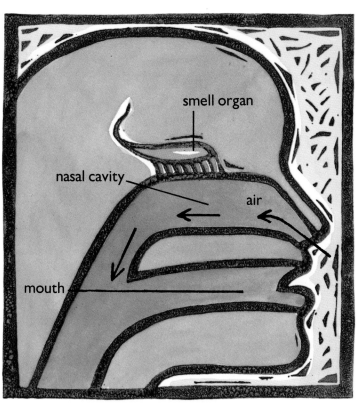

When you sniff, air is sucked into your nose. It passes over tiny hairs in the smell organ which trap any dirt and dust. When the air reaches the back of the nose, it passes over a sensitive **membrane** which sends signals to the brain. The brain interprets the signals as smells.

▼ How well can you smell? Blindfold a friend and ask him or her to identify a number of foods by sniffing them. You could ask her to smell substances such as orange juice, ginger, garlic, mustard and flour. Can she tell them apart? Mix two

of the substances together: can she still tell which is which? Who is the master sniffer in your group of friends?
Other things you could include in the smell test are slices of cucumber, lemon, roses, cheese, carrots or curry powder.

▲ Members of the dog family like these Arctic wolves, have noses a million times more sensitive than that of a person. This is partly because their noses are much longer and larger. Dogs use their sense of smell to find food and to distinguish between friends and enemies.

SCENT AND SAVOUR

Some people use their sense of smell at work. Professional wine-tasters buy in wine for supermarkets or shops. They sniff and sip many wines from different vineyards before making a choice.

Perfume makers can tell up to 10,000 different smells apart. With a cold, even they would find smelling hard, because the nose produces protective **mucus**, which blocks the nostrils.

Bath oil, stationery, perfume and foods often have nice-smelling **scents** added to make them more appealing. Many scents are made artificially. Most perfumes are distilled from natural sources like lavender, rose and jasmine petals. Some scents are used to repel: clothes moths keep well away from fabrics stored with moth balls.

▲ Have you ever noticed just how bad food smells when it begins to rot? This is nature's way of warning you not to eat food that could make you ill. **Bacteria** start to grow on old food and break it down, releasing the bad odour. You may see signs of mould too.

◀ Make a scratch and sniff card. Draw a shape on a piece of card then glue all sorts of smelly herbs, spices or talc on to different areas of the drawing. It should look quite colourful. Can your friends tell by sniffing exactly which substances you used? You could use the card for a special friend's birthday.

TASTE

Your tongue helps you to shape words, but it also allows you to taste and eat food. It is a muscle that can curl in all directions. It sorts and shapes food as you chew and swallow.

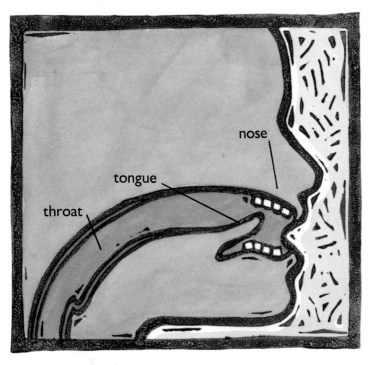

How many dry biscuits can you eat in a minute without drinking anything? To stop you from choking, **saliva** pours out of **glands** in your tongue and cheeks and mixes with food in your mouth to make a smooth, wet paste. Saliva also starts to digest, or break down, the food.

▶ Do you like eating seafood, like these mussels? Across the world, people enjoy eating a huge variety of different foods. Aboriginals in Australia love fat, white witchety grubs, which they eat fresh or toasted over a fire. Other delicacies people eat include chocolate-covered insects like locusts and grasshoppers, dried seaweed, frog's legs, snails and snakes. What food tastes best to you?

▼ These sticks of edible clay are eaten by some of the local people of Nigeria. The clay adds a valuable source of calcium to their diet. Calcium is a **mineral** used by our bodies to make bones, and to make and clot blood. We also need to eat a balanced mixture of other minerals, fats, vitamins, fibre and carbohydrates to keep healthy.

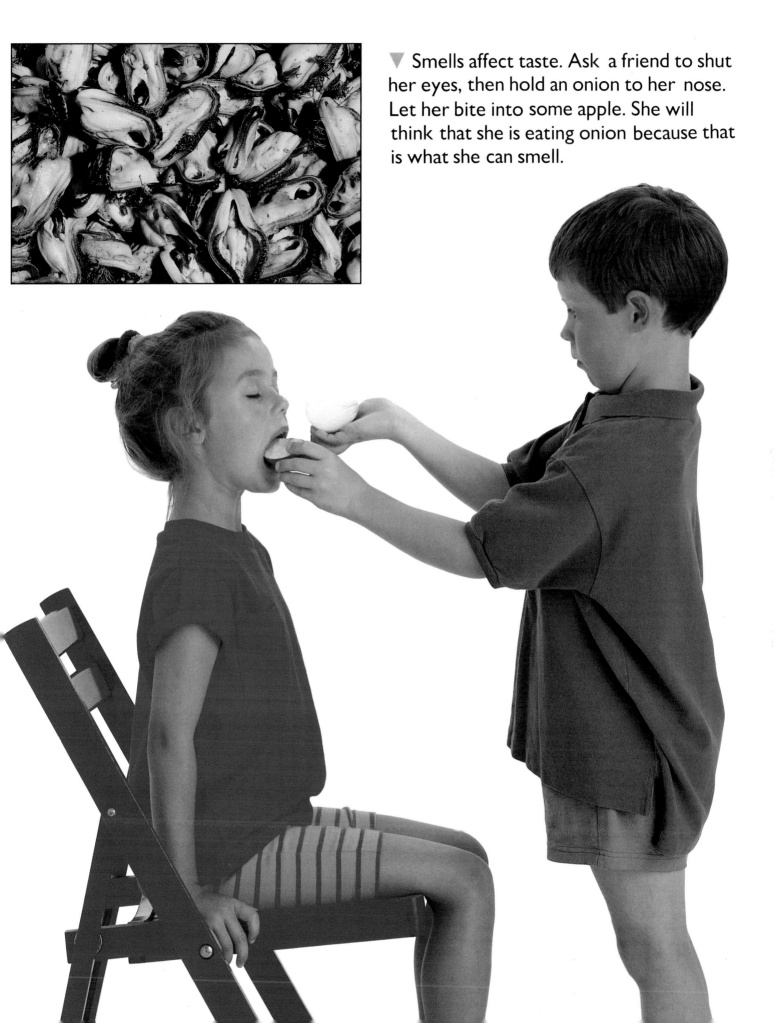

▼ Smells affect taste. Ask a friend to shut her eyes, then hold an onion to her nose. Let her bite into some apple. She will think that she is eating onion because that is what she can smell.

SWEET AND SOUR

Combinations of four basic tastes and thousands of different smells make up all the taste sensations you know from the things you eat and drink.

▼ How food or drink tastes is often influenced by its colour. Put drops of different food dyes into glasses of juice. Can your friends spot each fruity flavour, or are they put off by the colouring?

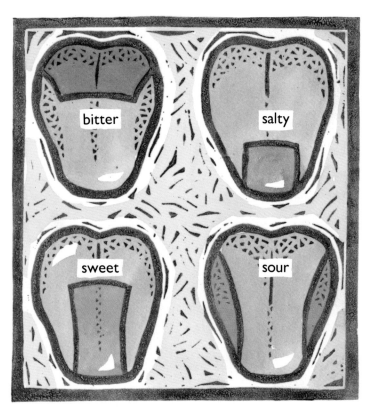

▲ Your tongue is covered with around 3,000 taste buds. These are tiny hollows in the tongue's surface, lined with taste-sensitive cells. There are four main types of taste: sweet, bitter, salty and sour. Groups of buds are better at sensing one type of taste than another. Messages pass from the buds along nerves to a special taste-centre in the brain.

▶ A toad extends its tongue to lick up an earwig. Its tongue can flick out and back again in one-tenth of a second.

▲ A hummingbird has a very long, thin tongue and beak to reach the sugary nectar right in the depths of a blossom. Hummingbirds eat substances very much sweeter than people can bear. They need a lot of energy to keep their hearts and wings beating rapidly.

TOUCH

Hot, cold, wet, dry, soft or prickly: sensors in your skin give your brain information constantly about the temperature and comfort of your body, and conditions in the world around you.

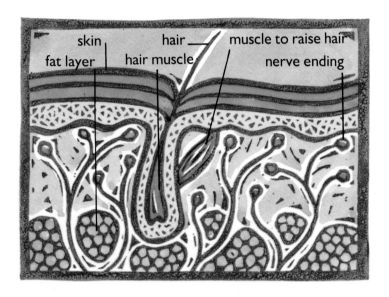

▲ A fly triggers touch-sensitive hairs on a Venus fly trap. Leaves will trap the fly, ready for the plant to digest.

▲ Skin is a thin layer covering your whole body. It is stretchy, so that when you move or grow, it moves and grows with you. Your skin is constantly being replaced. Millions of skin cells are lost from your body every day. Skin is oily, to keep you waterproof. On hands and feet, it is less oily, so it goes wrinkly if you stay too long in the bath. When you are hot, your skin produces sweat to keep you cool. When it is chilly, your hairs rise to trap a layer of warm air. All over your skin, nerve endings are at work, passing messages to your brain.

▲ Tickle a friend with a feather. Which areas of skin are the most sensitive?

▼ Every single person in the world has a unique pattern of tiny ridges on their finger tips. The police use fingerprint records to help track down suspects. Keep a file of the fingerprints of your family and friends. Press each finger tip on a stamp pad, then on to paper. Label each set of prints and keep your records safely in a folder.

▲ The colour of your skin depends on how much melanin it contains. Melanin is a pigment that helps to protect the skin against sunburn. People with white skin have little melanin. After a few days in the sun, their skin produces more melanin and develops a tan. People with darker skin have a lot of melanin.

21

HOT AND COLD

How sensitive are you? Lightly touch various areas of your skin with the points of a pair of tweezers. Which areas can sense both points? Mark the sensitive spots on a map of your body.

◀ Nerve endings in some parts of the body are much more sensitive to hot and cold than others. Do you dip your toe into the bath or swimming pool to test the temperature before you get in?

◀ Make a hole in the side of a box. Line up your friends and ask them one by one to put their hand into the box and to identify objects inside by touch alone. Who gets the most correct answers? Try touching objects with different textures such as a sponge, an orange, cold spaghetti, jelly, a hairbrush, a soft toy or the leaf of a plant.

▲ See how cold things affect your sense of touch. Put your fingers in a bowl of *melting* ice cubes for about 30 seconds. Now touch something very soft, and then something prickly. What do you feel? The cold of the ice cubes numbs your nerve endings so they do not send accurate signals to your brain.

Do not touch ice straight from the freezer, as it could burn your skin.

23

HEARING

What can you hear around you? Listen to the sounds when you rub your finger tips together next to your ear. What is the quietest sound you can hear?

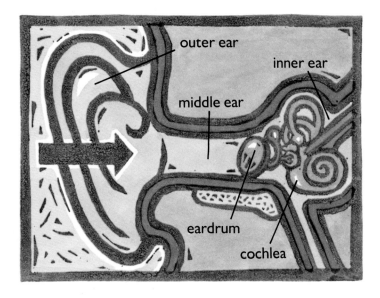

▲ The ear is made up of three parts. Sounds travel through the air in waves. They are received by the cup-shaped outer ear and directed into the middle ear. Here, **sound waves vibrate** a thin membrane, called the eardrum. Tiny bones in the middle ear vibrate, together with liquid in the **cochlea**. Nerves translate the vibrations into signals to the brain. The inner ear also helps the body to keep balance.

▼ Place rice or small sweets on a drum skin. Hold a baking tray above the drum and strike it. Sound waves will travel through the air, vibrating the drum skin like an eardrum and shaking the rice.

◀ Sound can travel through solid objects, like walls, or the ground. American Indians would put an ear to the ground to listen for riders.

▶ Dolphins communicate by sending high-pitched clicks through the water. They judge distances by the echoes that return. Dolphins can see and sense touch well but have no sense of smell.

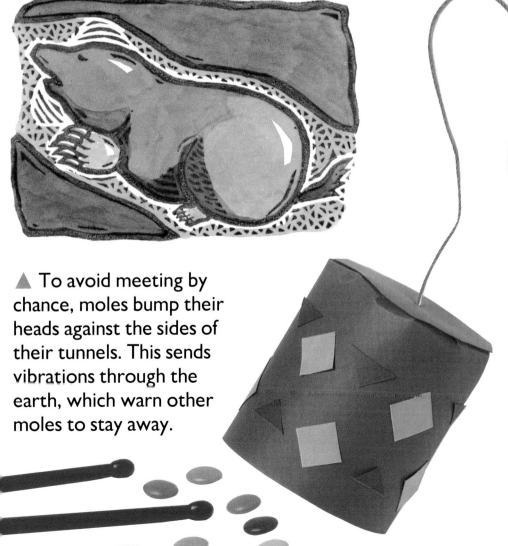

▲ To avoid meeting by chance, moles bump their heads against the sides of their tunnels. This sends vibrations through the earth, which warn other moles to stay away.

◀ Ask an adult to pierce a hole in the end of two yogurt pots. Push string through the holes and knot the ends so it does not slip through. Get a friend to hold one pot and then walk away to pull the string tight. Ask her to put her pot to her ear. Speak into yours. Your voice sets sound waves travelling along the string of your special telephone.

LOUD AND SOFT

Sounds are often pleasant, but some can cause harm. At a party or disco the noise may be so great that you later hear ringing in your ears. If so, your ears have suffered temporary damage.

▲ Large machinery used in industries like mining, or smaller equipment like some tractors or pneumatic drills can produce deafening sound levels. There are levels set by law in many countries, above which workers must wear heavy earphones to protect their ears. Too much noise present in the environment is called noise pollution.

▶ People and animals all hear sounds slightly differently. Your friend's favourite music may sound terrible to you. There are lots of sounds that are too high or low for people to hear. Sounds from dog whistles, and some bird, insect and bat noises are too high. We feel very low sounds as rumbling vibrations.

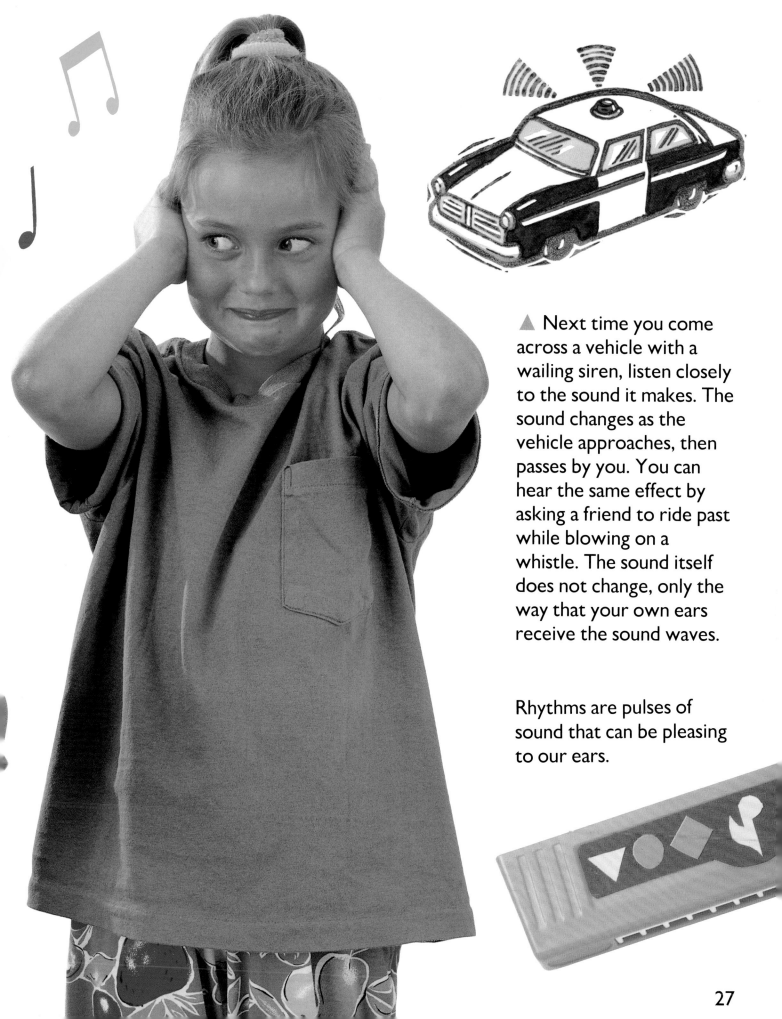

▲ Next time you come across a vehicle with a wailing siren, listen closely to the sound it makes. The sound changes as the vehicle approaches, then passes by you. You can hear the same effect by asking a friend to ride past while blowing on a whistle. The sound itself does not change, only the way that your own ears receive the sound waves.

Rhythms are pulses of sound that can be pleasing to our ears.

DIFFERENT WORLDS

Many people are born without full use of one or more senses, or lose them later through accident or illness. Their other senses may become sharper as a result.

▲ Many people wear contact lenses or spectacles. The extra lens alters the focus of light. Short-sighted eyes cannot focus on distant objects. Long-sighted eyes cannot focus on near objects.

THE BRAILLE SYSTEM

CELL

A B C D E

F G H I J

K L M N O

P Q R S T

U V X Y Z

▲ In 1829, a blind Frenchman called Louis Braille developed a system of reading and writing using raised dots, which are read with the finger tips. Braille is used all over the world. Language systems for people who are deaf involve signing with the hands, lip movements and writing.

As people grow older, their sense organs become less sensitive. They may use spectacles or a hearing aid.

Guide dogs are trained to act as the eyes of their blind owners. They wear a harness, which is held by the owner. They signal danger or whether it is safe to cross a road.

GLOSSARY

Bacteria are very tiny forms of life. They live in air, water, soil, and in and on plants and animals. Some bacteria cause disease in their hosts.

Brain receives input from the body's organs, stores memory, makes decisions and organises responses in the muscles.

Cell is a tiny piece of living matter. All living things are made up of cells.

Cochlea is a tube in the ear. It is filled with fluid and lined with tiny hairs. Sound vibrations move the hairs, which send hearing signals to the brain.

Gland is an organ in the body, such as sweat glands in the skin or tear glands near the eye. It either produces chemical substances or helps get rid of waste products from the body.

Roses

Iris is the coloured part of the eye.

Lens is the part of the eye that focuses light on to the retina. It is behind the iris.

Lungs are the two organs in your rib-cage, which draw air in and out to make you breathe.

Membrane is a very thin piece of skin or body tissue which joins or covers parts of a plant or animal.

Mineral is any substance that can be dug from the ground but is not plant matter. Calcium, iron and coal are all minerals.

Mucus is a slimy substance that is produced to protect delicate linings of the body. One sort forms in the nostrils when you have a cold.

Police car with siren

30

Nerves are long, thin cells, which run between organs all over the body. Sensory nerves carry messages from the sense organs to the brain. Motor nerves carry messages from the brain to the muscles, telling them what to do.

Pupil is the small, round hole in the middle at the front of the eye.

Listening to vibrations

Retina is the area at the back of the eye. It is light-sensitive and sends sight signals to the brain.

Right-handed is when a person finds most actions easier to perform with their right hand. The left side of the brain is larger in a right-handed person. The right side of the brain is the largest in left-handed people.

Saliva is the juice produced in glands in the cheeks and tongue, which helps you to mash food up and swallow it more easily. It also contains a chemical that starts to break the food down.

Scent is the particular smell of something, for example, the scent of baking bread or a wet dog.

Skin is the thin, elastic and waterproof layer that covers most of a person. It helps keep disease out from the insides.

Sound waves are the ripples through which sound carries through air, water or over solid objects.

Sweat is the salty liquid that comes from the skin to cool a body.

Vibrate is to quiver rapidly, to and fro. Sound travels as vibrations. A strong vibration can be powerful enough to knock down a building.

Red and green spectacles

INDEX